Harbours and Anchorages of Sc

C000058255

Contents

Harbours and Anchorages of Scilly
(1970: Revised 2018 and 2021)

These notes were prepared for our charterers in 1970. Since then, much has changed. Then, the only moorings available were in New Grimsby Sound and the private moorings inshore of the main jetty at Hugh Town, St Mary's. The latter, although the main harbour for the islands, was still an open anchorage exposed to the north-west and with indifferent holding. A north-westerly gale almost invariably produced chaos in the harbour and sometimes serious damage. Today, the harbour authority has laid many moorings there but still it can prove uncomfortable in a fresh or strong north-westerly. To my mind, there is only one anchorage in Scilly which may be protected in most conditions, namely St Helen's Pool although this can prove tricky of access and has an abundance of weed on the bottom which may give rise to indifferent holding (see below).

Otherwise, despite the proliferation of expensive moorings in some of the most favoured spots, there are a multitude of interesting anchorages which remain both free and attractive. However, with the possible exception of St Helen's Pool, none can be presumed safe in all weathers.

I have taken the liberty of leaving in the original notes contained in the Appendix. While tastes have changed over the years, and these notes may appear a little dated, the packing list may still serve as a useful aide-memoire when deciding what to bring while the catering advice may only be of interest to those who, like ourselves way back in the 70s, were a little short of the funds and could not afford the luxury of eating out regularly. Those were the days when the noticeboard outside Lloyds Bank in Hugh Town directed one to the nearest cashpoint in Broad Street, Penzance, and, while each island did have its own shop, supplies were very limited.

Today, each island is well supplied. Fresh bread, milk, vegetables etc. are readily available for those living on the island campsites or the rental cottages on Tresco. However, those reading these notes will, I hope be tempted to anchor some way from the nearest stores and your passage planning may well dwell upon the need to think about al fresco meals under the stars riding to anchor with maybe just one or two other yachts in the vicinity while the daytime visitors have all returned to the delights of Hugh Town or New Grimsby. For those who do want to eat ashore, I have included a brief section on restaurants and hotels serving meals. Most of the latter will allow you to partake of their showering facilities.

Finally, a word about water and diesel. This needs careful management and is only available by hose at St Mary's between 10.00 am (when the tripper boats leave) and 12 noon when the Scillonian arrives. It is best to fill up with both at either Penzance/Newlyn or Falmouth before leaving for the islands. In emergencies, water may be obtained by can either at St Mary's or on the quay at New Grimsby, or by asking at one of the off-island campsites. There is also a tap at the sanitation block above the quay at St Agnes.

Getting There

Most yachts going to Scilly, will make their departure from Falmouth. The distance is about 60 miles, easily covered in daylight hours during the summer months. However, tides need to be reckoned with, especially when rounding the Lizard. Ideally, departure from Falmouth should be made about one hour after HW Falmouth, but for various reasons this may not always be convenient. Given that the prevailing winds are from the west, the last thing you want is to be late at the Lizard so that you arrive at maximum ebb stream punching into a stiff southwesterly. This will set up a very nasty sea and necessitate going perhaps up to 7 or 8 miles offshore instead of gracefully rounding a few hundred yards off the outlying rocks off Lizard Point. Once clear you can make course for Scilly allowing the tide to push you clear of the Wolf Rock lighthouse which is right in the way.

Of course, should the wind be from the east, it should be an absolute doddle. Depending on the wind strength, it might be a little rough leaving Falmouth, but it will be glassy smooth rounding the Lizard and after that it is just a question of having the right amount of sail to maintain good progress. Probably, in an easterly, it is wise to enter the archipelago by going south-about St Mary's rather than attempting the shorter route over the Crow Bar. Just remember, that when the wind does come from the east, it tends to remain in that quadrant for some days, so don't plan to return from Scilly any time soon. It is great excuse to stay a little longer rather than returning to the office as planned.

If you have the time, it may be worthwhile taking two days for the trip. Given that the wind is more commonly in the west, or maybe the tides on the Lizard are not convenient, you have a number of interesting options. You have a greater flexibility of departure time in order to approach the Lizard just as the tide is about to turn in your favour. You will then be able to carry a fair tide all the way to your chosen overnight stop. Unless you want to do something unconventional, this stop is likely to be one of the following: Mullion (but only if the wind is settled from the east); St Michael's Mount, where you may anchor just to the west of the harbour entrance in reasonably settled weather (beware the rocky ledge running out from the shore on the west side); Penzance, with buoys just outside the entrance where you can wait for the lock to open into the totally sheltered inner harbour (but it can be uncomfortable on these waiting buoys in a fresh south-westerly); Newlyn which is available at all states of the tide, but may be crowded with fishing boats although now much more accommodating to yachts than it used to be (if full, or if you prefer, there is a good anchorage a few cables south of the entrance); and finally, Mousehole, where it is possible to anchor between St Clement's Island and the harbour in somewhat indifferent holding.

Finally, it is worth remembering that the prevailing westerlies are governed by depressions moving across to the north of the British Isles. This creates a constant fluctuation of the wind between the southwest quadrant and the northwest quadrant as the fronts pass through. If the wind backs to the southwest and you are tucked up in Penzance or Newlyn, it is much better to stay put and enjoy some wonderful fish and chips ashore in the sure knowledge that, within 24 hours or so, it will veer and bring better weather. When it does so, it may freshen up a little at first, but within an hour or so, the clouds will lift, the sky will turn blue and you will have a wonderful beam reach as you sail for six hours to these wonderful islands.

Arriving at Scilly

Thankfully, you don't need a visa, even though you do have to sail into the open Atlantic to get there. When you are about 11 miles off, the islands will start to appear. First, possibly the high isolated rock, Hanjague, which lies off the eastern isles, or maybe the very conspicuous daymark on St Martins. By now, you will have made your decision on whether to follow the deep-water channel, entering the islands by going south of St Mary's and thence either to the Cove on St Agnes or to St Mary's by way of St Mary's Sound or, instead, taking the shorter route over the Crow Bar.

If taking the former route, you must be aware of the Gilstone which covers at high water. The clearing marks are Line A (see page 5). However if unsure, once your latitude is less than 49° 54' N you will be sufficiently to the south of the rock, and can steer to clear Penninis Head by about a cable before rounding up into the Sound. If wishing to drop anchor in the Cove, you should continue to steer south west when past the Gilstone giving a good berth to the Spanish Ledges off St Agnes and other outliers southeast of the Gugh until you can see right up the middle of the Cove when you can turn in.

If going to the Eastern Isles, you will make towards Menawethan (see picture below) which you must round. (The neck between Menawethan and Great Ganilly is navigable but not recommended). There are extensive outliers to the west of Menawethan, but the east side of Ragged Island is clean. It is best to identify Ragged Island (which looks like its name suggests) and then head over towards it before turning in to the anchorage.

Menawethan (looking north)

If taking the short cut over Crow Bar to St Mary's, you need to make for the Hats Buoy which you must leave to Starboard. Be aware of the Biggal just south of Great Arthur and southwest of Menawethan, but once past it, you will be able to identify the Buoy and make for it in safety. Not only is the Hats Buoy the way into Crow Sound and St Mary's, but it is a useful starting point for 'running up the gun sight' into St Helen's Pool. And, if you want to stop, there is an excellent anchorage just a few cables due south of the buoy in Watermill Cove.

Hats Buoy

Crow Bar Bn.

Map showing approximate location of anchorages described in these notes

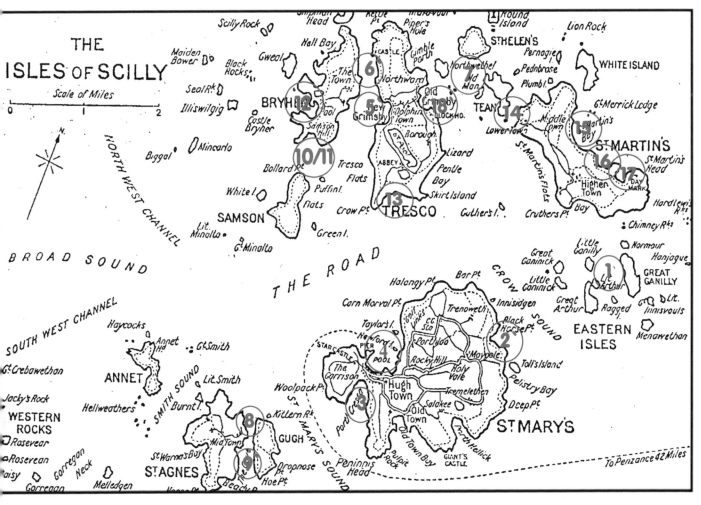

Aerial view of the islands

First - A Note on Transits

Despite GPS, the use of transits is vital especially when making up through narrow channels or 'necks' as they are often referred to in Scilly. You may experience sudden and unexpected tidal streams across your course and there may be little room for error. Scilly boatmen use many transits, but some of the most important are listed in below:

A. **Pidney Brow** (St Agnes) ⏀ **The Hoe** (Gugh) 241° (T) clears the **Gilstone** when rounding St Mary's from the South

B. **N Carn of Mincarlo** ⏀ SW edge of **Great Minalto** 307 ° (T) clears The **Woolpack** when coming up St Mary's Sound

C. **White Bns. on Mount Flagon** (St Mary's) 097 ° (T) lead into the harbour when coming from the south.

D. **Buzza Mill** (St. Mary's) ⏀ the **Black Stripe** on the seafront toilets 151 ° (T) leads into the harbour passing west of **The Cow**.

E. **Buzza Mill** ⏀ the end of the **lifeboat slip** 163 ° (T) leads into the harbour passing between **The Cow** and **The Calf**

F. **Babs Carn** (St Martins) ⏀ Pednbean 156 ° (T) leads west of **Black Rock** when entering **Tean Sound**

G. **Star Castle Hotel** (St Mary's) ⏀ $E.$ **Gap Rock** (St Helens) 182 ° (T) leads into **St Helens Pool** from the north. On near approach alter course to starboard to pass midway between **E Gap Rock** and **W Gap Rock.**

H. **Crow Rock Bn** ⏀ **Telegraph Tower** (St Mary's) 160 ° (T) leads **into Old Grimsby Sound** from the South. (near HW only).

I. **Hangman's Island** (New Grimsby Sound) ⏀ **Star Castle Hotel** (St Mary's) 157 ° (T) leads into **New Grimsby Sound** from the north

J. **Castle Bryher** (Bryher) ⏀ between the two summits of **Great Smith** (St Agnes) 35 ° (T) leads through **Smith Sound**

K. **St Helen's Carn** ⏀ the cleft in **Men-a-Vaur** leads in to **St. Helen's Pool** 316 ° (T) from the south (half tide upwards only)

Very rough sketch (c 1970) showing St Helen's Landing Carn in the cleft of Men-a-Vaur

1. Eastern Isles

A favourite fair-weather anchorage of mine (although hardly anyone else's!). It is very remote, but you can visit St Martin's with an outboard trip across the flats into **Highertown Bay** and there are huge pollack southeast of **Ragged Island** and the possibility of seals on smaller Eastern Isles. There are some interesting remains of Iron Age settlements on **Nornour**.

Enter from the south. Approach from a position just south of **Biggal** (the one south-east of Great Arthur), and identify **Ragged Island** to the north.

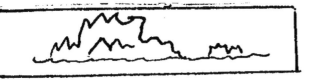

Ragged Island
(drawn from memory c. 1970)

Leave **Ragged Island** to port and enter the anchorage midway between it and **Great Ganilly**. Drop anchor, preferably on sand, on the **Ganilly** side of the anchorage and as far to the north-west as state of tides will allow.

Good shelter in reasonable weather except from the South East.

2. Watermill Cove

Excellent shelter and holding ground in gales from west or south-west but exposed to the east and south-east.

Make a position just south of the **Hats** buoy and enter the cove as far in as the state of tides will allow. Entrance should be made up the middle of the bay avoiding ledges of **Block House Point** to starboard and **Trenear's Rock** to port.

3. Porthcressa

Attractive, close to the town, and once again free now that the mooring buoys have been removed. Let's hope it remains an open and attractive anchorage. There is a fine beach with miniature gardens behind and landing on the beach you are immediately close to the shops.

Entrance is a little tricky (rocks scattered here and there) and Porthcressa is often crowded at the end of the day. You should be aware that Porthcressa is exposed to the south and any prolonged winds from that direction will produce an uncomfortable swell, especially around high water.

The dangers in the approach centre around the **Wras** which is joined at low tide to the Garrison forming a natural breakwater. Fortunately, a very small rock, (another Biggal!), always shows to the south of this group of ledges, but great care must be taken to avoid other ledges to the south-west of the Wras when approaching from the west.

Enter the anchorage about midway between the **Wras** and the rocks and ledges to starboard. Steer immediately for the flagpole in the northwest corner of the bay and drop anchor wherever you can find space and sufficient water away from the ledges to starboard and those closer in to the beach.

4. St Mary's Harbour

This is the main harbour for the town, St. Mary's and the islands as a whole. Nowadays, anchoring is only allowed outside of a line from the Pier Head to the Lifeboat and well clear of the area used by the Scillonian when entering or leaving her berth. The whole area inside this line, once a reasonably sheltered anchorage, is now filled with mooring buoys. These are designated by the size of the vessel using them and are charged accordingly. Although the harbour is reasonably sheltered in winds from the west through south to the north-east, it can be a little lively in a fresh north-westerly wind, and I would not remain there if there was a strong wind anywhere between west and north.

Approaching from the north and east, you should make a position approximately two to three cables west of the **Creeb Rocks** which lie about half a mile south-south-west of the **Crow Bar beacon**. On nearer approach to the pier head, the only danger is **the Cow**, which must be avoided below half-tide. This can be done by keeping outside of a line St Martin's daymark in transit with the summit of the Creeb rocks until the pier head bears south-south-east when steer for it.

Approaching from New Grimsby the correct line is with Star Castle bearing 157 degrees (T) until the leading beacons on the east side of the harbour come into line bearing 097 degrees (T). However, once past **Nut Rock** (a small isolated Rock close to starboard) it is ok to steer for the Pier Head ensuring that you do not get set to the east by wind or tide below half tide or you may encounter the Cow (see above).

Approaching from the south and west, you must give the Garrison a clearance of 2 to 3 cables in order to avoid all dangers, particularly when rounding the northwest corner of the Garrison. Once past **Steval**, the easternmost rock of the Garrison, it is best to steer greater than 20° by the compass until the harbour beacons come into line at 097 degrees (T) as above.

Landing is by dinghy at the dinghy pontoon at the root of the main pier. Fuel and water can be obtained alongside the outer pier by prior arrangement with the harbourmaster (Channel 12) and must be accessed after the departure of the tripper boats at 10a.m. and before the arrival of the Scillonian at 12 noon. There may be a number of yachts wishing to use the alongside berth at this time so do arrive promptly at the agreed time.

Lying just to the north of the designated mooring area and immediately to the south of **Taylor's Island** is a small, rocky cove which I have always called **Newlands Cove** but which is designated on the chart as **Porth Loo.** Here is a good anchorage for two or three yachts when the winds are between north-east through south to south-west. Be careful to anchor in sufficient depth as the underwater rocks inshore are steep-to and can give you a nasty bump in the night. A good position is a little west of south of the summit of Taylor's Island, but be careful not to obstruct the fairway of tripper boats passing between the Cow and the Calf.

You can land at the nearby beach or take the longer dinghy ride into the dinghy pontoon in the harbour (see above).

St Mary's Harbour

n season, all the moorings are filled, but in April, when this picture was taken, there is always plenty of room. Visiting yachts are moored to the right of the picture, well clear of the Scillonian berth and local boat moorings.

The strand at Hugh Town St Mary's, lies at the root of the jetty and inside local boat moorings. It is just below the Mermaid Inn and the Atlantic Hotel, where you can look out over the activity of the harbour while enjoying a beer or some lunch. The tall tower on the left is the power station chimney and to its right, the Buzza Tower which is an important transit mark when entering the harbour.

The 'Off-islands'.

Most day-trippers to the islands only get to see St Mary's, but the yachtsman can go where he pleases - mostly. Certain of the uninhabited islands including Annet and Roseveare, where I have landed previously are now bird sanctuaries and going ashore is not permitted.

Scillonians regard St Mary's as 'the Mainland', and the other four inhabited islands as 'the Off-islands'. Other islands (uninhabited) worth a visit are as follows: St Helen's, where there is a ruined pest house where returning sailors were quarantined with yellow fever and such, and the remains of a a 10th century chapel; and Samson whence the remaining population of 34 souls were forcibly evacuated in 1855. The remains of their stone cottages can still be seen.

The Four inhabited Off-islands are as follows:

Tresco is the second largest island, with a permanent population of around 600 (now only 175). The island is most famous for the Abbey Gardens which surround the home of the Dorrien-Smith family who have owned the island for generations. Tresco is now one large and very tasteful resort with timeshare accommodation and cottages to rent. There are three excellent eateries, the New Inn (by far the oldest of the three) at New Grimsby, the excellent Ruin Beach Cafe on the beach across at Old Grimsby, and the Flying Boat café, which I have yet to try and which serves breakfast as well as tea and coffee throughout the day. While the south of the island is well-developed, the north has remained wild and rugged and visits to Cromwell's Castle and King Charles' castle up on the hill provide some very scenic walking to get there.

Bryher lies across New Grimsby Sound from Tresco and is much wilder and less commercially developed. Here you will find tiny cottages surrounded by glorious flowers, dramatic views out to the west over the rock-strewn doorstep of the ocean and, at the end of the day a drink in the bar of the Hell Bay hotel.

To the south lies **St Agnes**, the smallest of the Off-islands with a population of about eighty, and the southernmost church in the UK. Walking inland from the quay, you may stop at the Turk's Head for a sharpener before reaching the Coastguard Café at the end of the road. Continuing further, you will emerge on to the downs and be rewarded with magnificent views across Smith Sound towards Annet and the Bishop Rock Lighthouse.

St Martin's with a population of about 140, has possibly some of the finest sandy beaches in the UK - and they are often deserted, even in summer. While you may come ashore in your dinghy at Lower Town and stop off at the St Martin's Hotel or the Seven Stones, the tourist boats come in across the flats to the quay below Higher Town where you will find the church, the island stores and, most remarkably, a world-class bakery which runs residential courses throughout the year.

Approaching the islands (approx. 7 miles out)

5 & 6 New Grimsby Sound

Reckoned by many to be the safest and best anchorage in Scilly. It is very pretty, close to some splendid pubs (on both Tresco and Bryher), but unfortunately, the best positions are usually taken! Buoys are now laid by Tresco Estate.

Although the approach from N is always possible and perfectly straightforward, it might be possible on the first visit to mistake the entrance to the E of **Shipman Head**. Therefore, you will approach for the first time from the South. This can only be done easily at half-tide or above — even local pleasure boats gave been known to get stranded on a falling tide hereabouts!

Steering to make good a course of 325 (T) from St Mary's, you will pass **Samson** on your port side. Formerly inhabited, the island was forcibly evacuated by the Dorrien-Smiths in 1855, although their ruined cottages can still be seen among the bracken which connects the twin hills of Samson which are un-mistakeably boob shaped.

 **Samson**

When the South Hill of **Samson** bears about due W, you will pass **Nut Rock** (see page 7) close to port. Ahead, you will then observe the **Hulman Bn**. easily, with **Rag Ledge Bn.** almost directly behind it.

Hulman Beacon

Rag Ledge Beacon

Steering an S-shaped course, you will round Hulman Bn about 1/2 cable to starboard then Rag Ledge Bn. about 1/2 cable to port. Once round Rag Ledge Bn steer 337 degrees (T) . Keep **Hangman's I.** (a steep sided pyramid shaped Isle in New Grimsby Harbour) just open of **Bryher.** When **Merrick I.** (a low islet directly on your course) is identified, turn to starboard and steer midway between it and **Plumb I.** to the E. whence proceed into the anchorage or head for the trot of moorings.

There are cables running between Tresco and Bryher just to the N of the Quay on Tresco. Their position is marked by triangular red marks on each side. You must anchor well clear either to the N or S of these cables. At neaps the best position is 1-2 cables to the W of the quay, but you will probably find insufficient water here at springs when you will have to find a suitable position (clear of the deep channel and rocks each side) S of Hangman's I. but N of the cables. For many reasons, neaps are much the best time for a visit to New Grimsby Sound; there is sufficient space to anchor inshore of the moorings just outside the harbour (position number 6) and even the moorings are more comfortable when the wind funnels through against the tide. The Moorings themselves are subject to strong tides around HW.

The quays on each of the islands are within easy reach of the anchorage position number 6, and you should visit the New Inn and Abbey Gardens on Tresco and The Hell Bay Hotel (for a drink and/or a super meal) on Bryher. Both islands are well worth exploring.

The distinctive twin hills of Samson are unmistakable. When visiting the island, it is best to land by dinghy near Puffin Island which lies on the north-east corner of Samson. It is possible to anchor just to the west of Puffin Island or further out on the south side of Rushy Porth, Bryher.

New Grimsby Sound looking north. To the left is Bryher, with Shipman Head at its furthest extremity. The yacht moored just to the left of Cromwell's Castle is on the line of moorings laid by the Tresco estate, which extends southward towards the jetty at New Grimsby.

Looking south. Hangman's Island is seen just to the left of Cromwell's Castle with the landing on Bryher just beyond. The Tresco Estate moorings are between Hangman's Island and New Grimsby.

7 St Helen's Pool

Another very interesting, if rather remote anchorage (although Old Grimsby and St Martin's can both be reached by o/b dinghy if you don't mind navigating through the surrounding rocks and islands).

Except at low tide, the anchorage can be approached from the N, but only when you have previously learned to identify **W. Gap Rock** and **E. Gap Rock**. (see p. 13)

The more usual approach is from the SE along Transit marked on the chart. Unless your pilotage is very secure, you should wait until there is plenty of water (say at least from 1/2 tide up, but more is better). From the east, you should steer to a position on the transit either close to the **Hats buoy,** or coming from St Mary's, to a position 3 cables S of **Guthers I.** This latter position can be reached by steering 1/2 mile NE form a position just N of **Crow Bn**.

If, for any reason, you cannot identify the leading marks from the position 3 cables S of Guthers I. **YOU SHOULD NOT PROCEED FURTHER**. However, these marks are conspicuous. (p.5 line K)

St Helen's Carn φ the cleft in **Men-a-Vaur**

It is **ABSOLUTELY ESSENTIAL** that you should hold these marks exactly until you reach the anchorage. As you proceed 'up the gun sight', you will observe many rocks and ledges both above and below the water - some perilously close!

When in the pool, turn a little to port and anchor about 1.5 cables S of Landing Carn to escape the worst of the tide.

8 & 9 St Agnes

Choose 8 or 9 depending upon prevailing wind. St Agnes is best for a day visit rather than an overnight stop unless the weather is very settled. If intending to lie off the quay in **Porth Conger**, beware of **the Cow** (another one!) immediately N. of the jetty. Give it a wide berth and approach from the NW. Anchor between the Cow and the jetty.

The Cove (just south of the bar between St Agnes and the Gugh which covers at HW) must be approached from the S keeping well clear of the dangers off the Garrison (described above under St Mary's). Then pass to the NE of the two buoys **Bartholomew Ledges** and **Spanish Ledges**) which mark the dangers on the SW side of St Mary's Sound. After rounding the Spanish Ledges, turn to starboard and sail for the southernmost part of St Agnes. Keeping 2 cables offshore on near approach. When you can see right up between St Agnes and the Gugh, turn into the Cove keeping to the middle. Anchor (according to tides) as far in as possible.

St Helen's Pool

This anchorage is, in my opinion, the only truly all-weather anchorage in Scilly. Here I have ridden out many a gale even from the northwest, which from the chart might seem exposed. However, the Golden Brow reef acts as a natural breakwater, and at high water, in a gale from that direction the breaking seas just a hundred yards or so from the anchorage are spectacular. I have seen spray flying sixty feet into the air while lying in relatively calm water just a few hundred yards downwind.

However, there is a lot of weed which can make setting the anchor a tricky business, but the clarity of the water is such that, even at high water, the bottom is clear and it is possible to seek out a relatively clear patch. If strong winds are forecast, it is advisable to row out in the dinghy (before the wind arrives!), and set a second anchor to create a moor having regard to the expected direction from which the wind will come.

The two pictures below show Moonshot anchored in the Pool on two different occasions. The top picture is looking north to the beach on the south side of St. Helens, while the second shows her neatly placed between the two Gap Rocks referred to in the text.

W. Gap Rk.   E. Gap Rk.

10 & 11 Rushy Bay and Samson

Neither of these anchorages were on my original notes, but I have used them quite frequently of late in settled weather. They are very beautiful, with great sunsets out to the western horizon and reasonable access by dinghy to both Samson and Bryher. Neither anchorage should be used if fresh or strong westerlies are forecast as they would become very exposed especially around high water.

The approach from the west is possible in deep water but requires careful pilotage through rocks entering from the North Channel south of **Maiden Bower** and **Illiswilgig** leaving **Mincarlo** to starboard.

A more usual approach is from **New Grimsby Sound** steering as for St Mary's until **Bryher South Hill** comes abeam, whence make a slow turn to starboard and enter the anchorage north of the **Rag Ledge** and **Hulman** beacons.

Coming from **St Mary's**, make as for **New Grimsby** (see above page 3) and when north of the **Rag Ledge** beacon, make course for **Bryher South Hill** and proceed as above.

Anchor in sufficient water south of **Bryher South Hill** or over on the **Samson** side of the sound between **Yellow Rock** and the shore. When making over to this side give Yellow Rock and its outliers a comfortable offing.

12 Stinking Porth, Bryher

In all but the most settled conditions, this is a dangerous anchorage with a difficult approach. However, I have used it a couple of times, and have been rewarded with magnificent sunsets over the western rocks and a real sense of seclusion. It also has the advantage of proximity to a really nice bar at the Hell Bay hotel where one may calm one's nerves after a nerve-wracking entrance through the narrow rocky entrance.

Approach is made through the western rocks keeping **Scilly Rock** on a bearing of 320 degrees (T) and leaving **Gweal Island** to port. Entrance should be made with great care on an ENE bearing, fending off any rocks that come too close.

13 Carn Near, Tresco

Not the prettiest anchorage but still beautiful (they all are!). A handy anchorage when everywhere else seems too crowded or expensive. Carn Near jetty has been re-built and is now the main landing place for visitors to the Abbey Gardens on Tresco. A useful overnight stop while awaiting an early morning departure over Crow Bar when the tide serves. Not a good place if there is any fetch from the south-west and wash from ferries can be a nuisance as the trippers arrive in the morning and depart around 5pm. After that, all is peace.

Approach from St Mary's towards Carn Near is made on a course of 335 degrees (T) leaving **The Mare** and other rocks and ledges close to starboard on near approach

Anchor clear of **Figtree Ledge** in a position a little to SE of the jetty but taking care not to obstruct the ferries.

14 Tean Sound

The hotel on St Martin's maintains some moorings in the sound and in the past has provided splendid meals and welcome showers when we have visited. The hotel is now managed by a new company providing specialised holidays as the Karma Hotel. Food is served, but no longer alas in the superb upstairs room with amazing views. The hotel, together with a few cottages, is known as Lower Town and, as you walk along St Martin's single roadway, do not miss the Seven Stones pub up the hill on your left a few yards along from the hotel. It is a wonderful place with amazing views, fantastic food and good Cornish beers.

Like so many of the inlets in the north of Scilly, you must come in from the north if you do not want your arrival time to be dictated by the tide. Make a position about 2 cables north-east of the lighthouse on **Round Island** being careful that you are not swept eastward by the tide on to the **Deep Ledges** to port. Then make good a course of about 145 degrees (T) towards **Tinklers Point** which forms the southern extremity of the little bay to port. This leg of the approach is nearly a mile in length and from start to finish there are **dangerous underwater ledges** on your port side. When you are about 1 cable off the point you will be able to see the moorings and fishing boats moored in the sound and you should make towards them trying to keep about midway in the channel.

From the south you will need a good rise of tide and excellent pilotage as you make your way from the **Crow Bar** beacon northward across **St Martin's Flats** and the maze of rocks and shoals that lie in wait for the unwary as they attempt this approach to **Tean Sound** (pronounced Tee-an) without local knowledge. I have done it - but it is not really advisable for those of us who are merely visitors.

15, 16 and 17 Bays on the North side of St Martins

St Martin's island is renowned for its extensive and deserted silver beaches. There can be few beaches in the UK that can rival those that lie on its northern shores. In reasonable weather, with sunshine and not a trace of north in the wind you will anchor in paradise. Remember however that things can change fast in Scilly; with fierce tidal streams in the offing, a vicious sea can build up in moments should the wind veer into the northerly quadrant. So, unless you are very sure of conditions, this is not a place to stray too far from your ship and you should be prepared for a quick getaway by day or night.

There are only shoal draft anchorages on the south side of the island. Landing is best made on the west of the Island by the slipway below the hotel at **Lower Town**. This is in **Tean Sound**, but is reachable by an interesting dinghy ride through the rocks from the anchorage in St Helen's Pool.

In the past, the hotel has, on several occasions, supplied showers and a splendid meal in the upstairs restaurant with stunning views over the rocks and shoals of northern Scilly. Here, in its early days the hotel provided a wonderful winter honeymoon for Judith and me. However, the hotel has now changed hands and although on my last visit, the staff were friendly and welcoming I noted that the restaurant had moved downstairs while the glorious upstairs room was being used by salesman selling Karma holidays.

There are three possible anchorages on the north coast provided the winds are not onshore. All three need care on approach due to off-lying rocks and fast tidal streams. They are (from east to west):

Stony Porth. Approach from NE or NW taking care to avoid the **Tearing Ledges** which lie to the north of the anchorage.

Bulls Porth. This needs great care in the approach. Make a position some two or three cables to the west of the **Tearing Ledges** and enter on a SSW heading leaving **Murr Rock** to port and the **Santamana Ledges** to starboard.

St Martin's Bay. A truly wonderful place in summer when the sun shines on the silver sands of what must be one of the finest and least populated beaches in the UK. Unfortunately, it is the most difficult to enter due to the numerous rocks and islets in the approach.

Enter on a S bearing leaving the **Merrick Rocks** 150 metres to starboard and the **Mackerel Rocks** 150 metres to port. Once in, you may anchor in 3 metres sand, and enjoy a well-earned gin and tonic to still the adrenaline rush.

18. Old Grimsby, Tresco

This part of Tresco is gentler than New Grimsby, and much quieter although none of Tresco could be classed as noisy - cars are forbidden on the island and transport is by tractor driven bus. Here there is a little quay for landing, and the island primary school, with its handful of children, enjoys a situation just yards away from a beautiful sandy beach. Beware though! This idyllic setting masks a treacherous approach and some nasty surprises. Anchoring on a sandy beach in a catamaran many years ago to dry out, I awoke to find that we were resting most comfortably on soft sand but had swung to within inches of an enormous rock which had parked itself right next to us.

From the north, the approach is reasonably straightforward although exposed to any significant swell from the northwest. From a position about three cables north of **Kettle Rock** and its swirling outliers and overfalls to the north of Tresco, proceed on a bearing of 122 degrees (T) leaving the north of **Tresco** about 1 cable to starboard and making for a position about midway between **Tresco** and **Northwethel**. From here, you may turn slightly to starboard but keeping to mid-channel until **Old Grimsby Harbour** comes abeam when you can anchor as far in as tidal depth will allow to escape the worst of the stream which is fierce at times near HW. Shelter is generally good, but may be a little rolly around HW, and distinctly unpleasant in a fresh north-westerly.

It may be a little quieter to proceed further in, continuing up mid-channel until the beacon on Rushy Point comes abeam. Be careful to avoid anchoring near the Westward Ledge which extends to the west of the Little Cheese Rock, and also the marked cable connecting the islands of Tresco and St Martin. This anchorage is likely to be completely deserted; beyond it are the Tresco Flats which dry, exposing a nasty rash of rocks at LW. However HW will allow you to proceed further south across Tresco Flats on to the Crow Bar beacon and St Mary's.

NB All the drawings are impressions from memory and date from about 1970!

David Eastburn - April, 2021

Tresco

Top:
King Charles' Castle

Centre:
Old Grimsby

Bottom:
Carn Near anchorage

Where to Eat?

St Mary's

There are multiple places to eat in Hugh Town plus several scattered elsewhere on the island. Be warned that in the season many are fully booked so it is best to ring first. Obviously, I have not eaten in them all, and I guess there are some excellent ones I have missed. However, I can say that I have never been disappointed. For an authentic pub atmosphere, I can recommend the **Atlantic** (01720 422417) and the **Mermaid** (01720 422701). The latter has a family room which lacks atmosphere but is conveniently close to the quay. For scenery - well all are pretty good, but I love **Juliet's Garden** (01720 422228) above the anchorage at Porthloo. Posh meals are available at **Tregarthens** (01720 422540) and, if you don't mind the walk, excellent lobster is to be had at the **Longstone** (01720 422410) in the middle of the island. (They will also deliver if you can arrange a convenient meeting spot ashore.)

St Agnes

The Turks Head (01720 422434) is conveniently close to both the Cove Anchorage and Porth Conger. It is absolutely essential to book as far ahead as possible if you want dinner ashore. Pub grub is served to all and sundry at lunch time when the tourists abound. Up on the hill at the end of the track is the **Coastguard Café** (01720 423747) which serves excellent food. Once again booking is a must as space is limited.

Bryher

Food obtainable at the bar in the **Hell Bay Hotel** (01720 422947) - and no, you don't have to dress for dinner, shorts will do - or in the dining room. Advisable to book. We have eaten in the **Fraggle Rock** (01720 422222), the last outpost as you move north along the east side of the island. The menu is limited but the experience is wonderfully laid back.

Tresco

The New Inn (01720 423006) has long been the favoured watering hole for yachtsmen visiting Tresco. There is a swimming pool and with a bit of negotiation a shower may be available. Over at Old Grimsby on the other side of the Island is the superbly sited **Ruin Beach Cafe** (01720 424849),where I have spent many a happy hour while younger crew members have been off exploring.

St Martin's

The St Martin's Hotel (01720 422368) at Lower Town, is very convenient if you are moored or anchored in Tean Sound. Be aware, though, that the tide runs fiercely past the stone jetty which is regularly used by the tripper boats and ferries. So fond was I of this hotel in the old days, that we chose to have our honeymoon here some 30 years ago. It is now run by the Karma group and, sadly, we found recently that the splendid upstairs dining room, which has one of the finest views in all Scilly, had been converted into a sales venue while food was served downstairs. There are showers and changing rooms just inside the hotel entrance which the friendly staff allowed us to use on our last visit. Just 50 yards up the road from the hotel, is a footpath leading up to the Seven Stones Inn (01720 423777) which serves good pub grub either inside or on rough-hewn benches and tables al fresco. Higher town, about a mile up the road, is the main hub of island life. Here, Adam's Fish & Chips (01720 423082) is open most of the day while a pleasant afternoon cuppa may be had in the Little Arthur Café which also opens on Wednesday and Friday evenings.

APPENDIX

1. WHAT TO BRING - suggested inventory (prepared for all who sail anywhere with us)

The following suggested inventory is not prescriptive, but may be of some use. It has been developed over some 50 years of arranging this sort of venture!

Please do not bring your kit in a suitcase or framed rucksack. Use a kit-bag or hold-all if possible. Polythene bags for storing bedding, spare underclothes etc., make the best use of storage space and will ensure that the contents remain dry. Avoid bringing unnecessary gear as space is very limited, but do not skimp on spare warm clothing as, even in summer, it can be very cold at sea.

:Passport
EH1C card* and/or travel insurance
Euros (if available — but you can always change English money or use a card in France)
Sleeping bag (or duvet plus sheet)
Pillow
Waterproof jacket and trousers (please let me know if you want to borrow a set)
Spare warm clothes/underclothes
Soft shoes/trainers (black-soled shoes should not be worn on deck)
Spare pair ditto &/or sailing wellies
Nightwear
Washing gear, toothbrush & towel
Neck scarf/small towel (to stop drips running down inside your clothes in wet weather)
Swimming gear
Sun block
Sun Glasses
Books/games/knitting
Camera & film
Torch (& batteries)
Favourite seasickness remedy (Stugeron recommended)
Elastoplasts etc.
RYA log book (if applicable)

You may also wish to bring a scrap book or exercise book to make a diary or log book of the cruise.

(Items in red not required for cruising in UK waters)

----

2. FAMILY VICTUALLING (FALMOUTH - SCILLY - FALMOUTH)
2-13 June, 2016. 3/4 people (Total = 10 days. 35 meals)

LUNCH X 9

BREAKFAST X 10

Menu:

Menu:

Porridge or Cereal
Fruit Juice
Bread/Toast and Marmalade
Tea/Coffee
Eggs
Bacon
Tomato

2 X Lentil Soup
2 X Fish soup
Fresh caught fish
Bread and butter/margarine
Fruit
Chocolate biscuit

Plus one (or more) of following:

1. Cheese (4 days)

2. Pate/Cold meat (6 days)

DINNER X 9 (+ Cliffside BBQ June 3)

Menu:

1. 4 pork loin with mushrooms, 4 tomatoes, 12 small potatoes and green veg (brocolli?)
2. Roast Chicken (plus 12 small Potatoes and green veg, beans?)
3. Cold chicken salad. (1 lettuce, 4 tomatoes, ½ cucumber, 1 carrot, celery, 12 small potatoes, mayonnaise/pickle.
4. Pork a la Manche
5. Spaghetti Milanese*.
6. Chilli con carne (tinned meat, tinned kidney beans, tin sweetcorn, chilli powder rice) OR Fish pie (depending on catch)
7. Spaghetti bolognese
8. 12-16 sausages, 12 small potatoes, tinned peas
9. 4 steak, 12 small potatoes, frozen peas

PUDDINGS

1. Fresh fruit
2. 2 steamed puddings
3. 4 yoghurts
4. 4 yoghurt or similar
5. tinned fruit and custard
6. tinned fruit and custard

SNACKS

Instant hot chocolate	= 1 jar.
Biscuits	= 6 packets
Squashes	= 1 lemon squash
	= 1 orange squash.

3. SHOPPING LIST BEFORE DEPARTURE

Cereals etc
1 pkt porridge oats
1 pkt muesli
2 loaves stayfresh sliced bread

Drinks
8 pks tea
pks cafetiere coffee
bottle orange squash
bottle lemon squash
L fresh squeezed orange juice
L long-life orange juice

Dairy
2 dozen eggs
36 slices bacon
1 pkt butter
1 medium tub olive spread or similar
2 large cheddar cheese – (2 kinds?)
8 yoghurts or similar
2L fresh semi-skimmed milk
2L long-life milk

Fruit and Vegetables
0 tomatoes
6 portions fruit (satsuma/apple/banana)
lemons
largish bags potatoes
large bag onions
portions green veg (suggest 3 portions green beans + 3 brocolli or similar)
pair lettuce (little gem, romaine or similar
cucumber
carrots (from home)
mushrooms
bulbs garlic

Poultry and meat
12 portions cold meat/pate
(1 large or 2 small
slices=1 portion!)
4 nice steaks
4 pork chops(for pork a la Manche)
1 cooked chicken
4 pork loins (for frying)
12/16 sausages
1 minced beef

1 jar mayonnaise
1 jar pickle
2 tins stewed steak or similar
1 tin kidney beans
1 tin baked beans
1 tin peas
1 medium tin stewed steak
2 tins tuna fish
1 tin sweetcorn
4 (3) tins tomatoes
2 tins steam pudding
1 jar chilli powder
2 tins fruit salad mix
1 jar hot chocolate
1 jar marmalade
1 jar jam
1 small bottle cooking oil
1 small bottle wine vinegar
1 jar mayonnaise
1 jar sweet pickle

Dried/Instant foods etc

18 sachets instant soup various fla
vours
2 pkt spaghetti
24 club biscuits or similar
6 packets assorted biscuits
2 pkt cream crackers or other dry
biscuit
1 pkt mixed herbs
1 pkt curry powder
1 pkt chilli powder
1 pkt oxo cubes
1 small pkt flour
1 pkt rice
Chocolate
2 bags dried fruit
1 pkt instant custard
Chocolate
2 bags dried fruit
1 pkt instant custard

ALCOHOLIC BEVERAGES etc

1 Bottle whisky
1 bottle gin
8 x cans lager
4 X cans Guiness
12 pkts crisps/nuts
3 bottles tonic

CLEANING

6 (2) Loo rolls
small Bin liners
Plastic bags
Jif cream cleaner
Washing-up liquid
Air-freshener

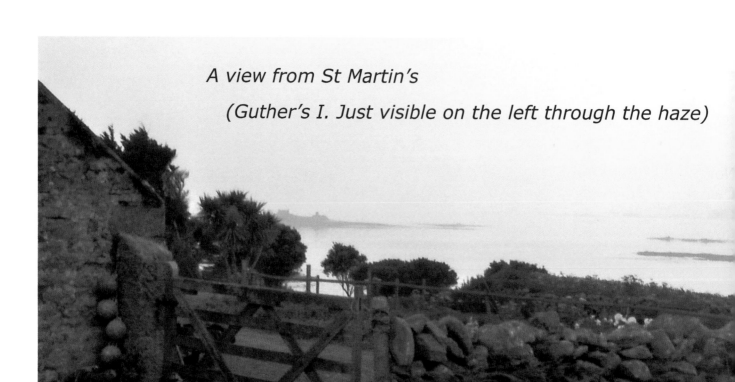

A view from St Martin's

(Guther's I. Just visible on the left through the haze)

Also by David Eastburn
Innocents in India

Not willing to pay tour companies to provide a standard tour of the must-see sites, David and Judith Eastburn decided to arrange their own six-week adventure a little off the beaten track. The results were usually unexpected, frequently a little challenging but always full of excitement and nearly always great fun. Their accommodation varied from desert sand to a royal palace and their journeys did not always turn out as expected.

This account of two novice travellers is a light-hearted tale, lavishly illustrated, and strongly recommended reading for those readers who may be contemplating a do-it-yourself visit to this vibrant and colourful country.

Available from Amazon, Published by Blurb © David Eastburn 2016